Introduction by W. Terrence Gordon

A full decade before he published *Understanding Media*, McLuhan offered the readers of *Explorations Two* (1954) this embryonic version of the book, and many of its key insights. Between the present essay and *Understanding Media*, he would say for the first time that the medium is the message; here the same principle is articulated at the end of his opening paragraph as a corollary to his observation on the widespread inattention to communication as involvement in a shared siutation: "[I]t leads to ignoring the *form* of communication as the basic art situation which is more significant than the information or idea 'transmitted.'" And so the theme announced in the title, the link between medium as message and art forms, is established and opens the way to the manifold illustrations of the link in the text that follows. Even before this valuable paraphrase and expansion of basic McLuhan are introduced, his opening sentence ("The use of the term 'mass media' has been unfortunate.") is an explicit caution against the excessively narrow view of media to which commentators would fall prey in discussing *Understanding Media*. As is the case for all the essays assembled in this collection, careful and reflective reading is repaid by insights gleaned from McLuhan's reworking of his themes: "Every medium is in some sense a universal, pressing toward maximal realization. But its expressive pressures disturb existing balances and patterns in other media of culture." Among the condensed riches of this brief essay, it is possible to detect a preliminary formulation of a notion that would ultimately appear as the principle of reversal in McLuhan's posthumously published *Laws of Media*: "The intensely abstract character of the printed page was to be the matrix of the technology of America. But paradoxically, the new technology was to produce a new set of arts and a new architecture which was anything but abstract." — WTG

Notes on the Media as Art Forms

The use of the term 'mass media' has been unfortunate. All media, especially languages, are mass media so far at least as their range in space and time is concerned. If by 'mass media' is meant a mechanized mode of a previous communication channel, then printing is the first of the mass media. Press, telegraph, wireless, telephone, gramophone, movie, radio, TV, are mutations of the mechanization of writing, speech, gesture. Insofar as mechanization introduces the 'mass' dimension, it may refer to a collective effort in the use of the medium, to larger audiences or to instantaneity of reception. Again, all of these factors may create a difficulty of 'feedback' or lack of rapport between 'speaker' and audience. There has been very little discussion of any of these questions, thanks to the gratuitous assumption that communication is a matter of transmission of information, message or idea. This assumption blinds people to the aspect of communication as participation in a common situation. And it leads to ignoring the *form* of communication as the basic art situation which is more significant than the information or idea 'transmitted'.

At many levels, printing established a divorce between 'literature and life' which was scarcely heard of before printing and which is meaningless today when print is recessive, on one hand, or mainly pictorial in impact, on the other. The well-established view of culture which assumes that it filters down from *élites* to popular levels will not stand up for a moment to the facts of linguistic history and formation. Yet language is the great collective work of art transcending all individual works. Today this naive content-view of culture prevents us from directing serious critical attention to the media, old and new, as art forms. It is a charley horse inhibiting all education in a technological society.

Today the advance of TV as a communication channel helps us by contrast to focus some of the basic features of cinema. The very word 'Hollywood' suggests the sacred grove from which has issued in our century a new pantheon. The power of the movie projector to evoke gods and goddesses is not accidental. On one hand, there is the movie camera with its analytical power to arrest, dissect, and record motion. The camera rolls up the carpet of existence. On the other hand, the projector reconstructs the dissected scene and unrolls the daylight world as a magic carpet, a dream-world. The camera records the day-world; the projector evokes the night-world. The daylight world intensified by the 45 degree vision of the camera reveals on the dark screen its obverse. The movie patrons assemble in the 'cave' to observe the shadows of the phenomenal world as projected by the dreaming eye of the movie god. Plato and Hollywood join hands in a metaphoric dance on the sands of California.

The spatial image offered by camera eye and projector has a peculiar limitation. It tends to by-pass everything in existence characterized by routine, repetition and continuous effort. Like the short story or the lyric poem, cinema works best with the single mood, state of mind, or metaphor. These it can elaborate or sustain for minutes or hours. The transforming magic of the short poem and short story appear as unexpected associates of camera-eye as an art form. And cinema would seem to be closely related to the romantic art of the esthetic moment, the moment of arrested attention. As Christopher Caudwell put it in *Illusion and Reality*: 'There is a poetic instant and as time vanishes, space enters; the horizon expands and becomes boundless. The art reveals itself as double.'

It is the technological equivalent of the process by which we recreate within ourselves the exterior world. The artist arrests his cognitions by recognition. He then reverses the process and embodies in an exterior work the drama of apprehension. The stages of apprehension, reversed and embedded in new matter, enable us to contemplate, purge and dominate the drama of cognition, the dance of existence. This reversal leading to contemplation is a catharsis. But this is precisely the action of camera and projector *vis-à-vis* the visible world. So that anything whatever taken up into this seemingly banal mechanical process is nevertheless metamorphosed. Here it is possible to suggest an answer to the mysterious question raised by Sigfried Giedion in *Mechanization Takes Command*. In his masterly account of the mechanization of the bread industry he expressed bewilderment at the fact that European immigrants accustomed to excellent bread were in America eager for the ersatz loaf. The answer lies in the fact that we are also eager for ersatz dreams, blondes, houses and entertainment. Is it not the sheer magical power of the technological environment which leads us to prefer the artificial to the natural? Bread in the first place is a product of art. But when the entire economy is on an artistic or magical basis, sparked by the magical appeals and promises of the ads (visual ads are in themselves magical in their habit of transforming ordinary objects and situations) is it not repugnant to the total pattern and promise of the new life to accept 'natural' effects even at the level of physical taste? The power of the machine to transform the character of work and living strongly invites us to transform every level of existence by art. In a collective way we seem to have followed the esoteric counsels of Baudelaire 'sur le maquillage' in seeking by art to rediscover an Edenic world.

Gilbert Seldes mentions how in the early days of TV crowds would stand by the hour watching a TV screen in a shop window when the only picture on the screen was of the traffic in the street in which they stood. Such is likewise the magical power of the press. Reportage takes up the ordinary events, the weather and the municipal events in which we all participate, and changes them simply by virtue of the medium of print and photography. Any communication link or channel necessarily possesses this mythic dimension. Much more are the ineluctable modalities of sight and sound charged with powers of metamorphosis which have been magnified by technology into the size and posture of mighty djinns.

The TV camera is not the movie camera. It does not arrest the flow of action in a series of still shots. Its continuous pick-up is like the radio mike with respect to the voice. Again the TV screen is not the movie screen. In some sense the spectator is himself the screen. The cathode tube carries 'the charge of the light brigade'. The tube carries both the charge and the answering barrage. The result is the painting of images by the ballet of electrons. Again, the small screen and the small audience of TV completely alter the relation of image to external world and to audience.

As Erasmus was the first to grasp the character of the revolution of the printing-press, James Joyce was the first to exploit the multiple revolution of telegraph, press, radio, cinema, and TV. *Finnegans Wake* has already begun to appear as an orchestration of all the media of communication, ancient and modern. And it was his mastery of the art process in terms of the stages of apprehension that enabled Joyce to install himself in the centre of the creative process. Whether it appears as mere individual sensation, as collective hope or phobia, as national myth-making or cultural norm-functioning, there is Joyce with cocked ear, eye and nose at the centre of the action. He saw that the change of our time ('wait till Finnegan wakes!') was occurring as a result of the shift from super-imposed myth to awareness of the character of the creative process itself. Here was the only hope for a world culture which would incorporate all previous achievements. The very process of human communication, Joyce saw, would afford the natural base for all the future operations and strategies of culture. Towards this vivisectional spectacle of the human community in action we have been led ever more swiftly in recent decades by increasing self-consciousness of the processes and effects of the various media of communication. Our knowledge of the modes of consciousness in pre-literate societies together with our sense of the processes of culture formation in many literate societies past and present, have sharpened our perceptions and led to wide agreement that communication itself is the common ground for the study of individual and society. To this study Joyce contributed not just awareness but demonstration of individual cognition as the analogue and matrix of all communal actions, political, linguistic and sacramental.

What Erasmus saw was that the printed book was to revolutionize education. He saw that the book gave new scope and power to the classroom. What we have to see is that the new media have created classrooms without walls. Just as power technology has abolished 'nature' in the old sense and brought the globe within the scope of art, so the new media have transformed the entire environment into an educational affair.

Concentrating briefly on one aspect of photography as it revolutionized painting technique as well as the conditions for contemplation of art, André Malraux came up with his news of 'museums-without-walls'. The main force making in that direction he saw was the clarification of the painter's medium itself. The canvas gradually freed from anecdote and narrative became in our time not a vehicle but sheer expression. This was the heritage of Cézanne, whose concentration on one formal problem ('the realization of space by the juxtaposition of areas of pure color') led to a break-through as spectacular as that of Planck and Einstein. But this discovery occurred simultaneously in poetry and music. And it enables us to see that each channel of expression (even press, radio, cinema) awaits a similar day of emancipation. Every medium is in some sense a universal, pressing towards maximal realization. But its expressive pressures disturb existing balances and patterns in other media of culture. The increasing inclusiveness of our sense of such repercussions leads us today hopefully to investigate the possibilities of orchestral harmony in the multi-levelled drive towards pure human expressiveness.

Erasmus, the text-book, and the Renaissance classroom constitute a subject for meditation related to the interaction of the printed page as new art form and the older cultural equilibrium between manuscript and oral communication. The Renaissance classroom was transferred to America minus the manuscript tradition and conversation minus the plastic milieu of European art and architecture. The intensely abstract character of the printed page was to be the matrix of the technology of America. But paradoxically, the new technology was to produce a new set of arts and a new architecture which was anything but abstract. Yet the original trauma of cultural translation from old to new world has remained.

In this century, however, we have seen James, Pound and Eliot revolutionizing the verbal culture of Europe by their technological impact on the old world. And contrariwise, we have had LeCorbusier and Giedion verbalizing our technological culture. Here it would seem is the formulated means of healing the wounds caused in our Western culture at the Renaissance.

North American children respond esthetically to the powered objects in their world. Streetcars, locomotives, airplanes and motorcars are the first objects of delighted contemplation. But in the classroom the student is confronted with verbal culture in book form. For the European, on the other hand, verbal culture is as much an object and area of spontaneous delight and play as machinery for us. The conclusion is obvious. We can master verbal culture and European art only by approaching it *at first* as a technical problem, just as some Europeans have mastered our sports, jazz, machinery, and architecture by translating it into their verbal cultures. Once the bridge has been crossed in either direction the bridge is no longer necessary. It functions only as a grammar and crib in early stages of reading a new language.

But such temporary bridges are necessary today not only between cultures but within our own culture as a means of mastering the different languages of sight and sound spoken by the new media of communication. It is not only at the political level that we have to know several languages. Locked up for four centuries in the dominant language of the printed page, we unconsciously attempt to handle all communication problems in its rectilinear, form-content language. So unconscious are we of this problem that we have even lost the ability to read the printed page through the sheer distraction created by the other media. Many people have noted how ours is an 'eye-minded' culture. But we do not have educated eyes. Similarly our ears are assailed by messages as no ears have ever been assailed, but we do not have educated ears.

The printed page has blinkered us until we have lost the clues to the nature of communication and its relation to the art process.

Such a view would seem to provide a solution to 'the case of the missing anecdote'. In *Encounter 4*, a student at the University of Utah recorded the conversation between Dylan Thomas and some members and students in the Department of English. That record is worth all the critical essays that have been written on Thomas. Thomas poured out stories, comments and observations during his tours. So have many other poets and artists. But nobody has seen fit to record them. The spoken word we seem to regard, along with our own popular culture, as illegitimate, not really culture. Europeans, on the other hand, unparalyzed by the art-form of the book, have always allowed great cultural and literary value to the anecdote, the chance remark and the 'first acquaintance' with a poet or painter. Here they expect to see the mind of the artist in spontaneous action, just as they seek in conversation to awaken and rally creative resources.

In this regard the pocketbook can be seen as a form which exorcises the cultural bogey of the book. Cheapness and convenience are scarcely the clues to the success of the pocketbook today. Rather, as Delmore Schwartz suggested in the *New York Times Book Review* (Jan. 17, 1954): 'The pocket book reader's only desire is pleasure and he is not likely to be suspected of being an intellectual and a highbrow, as he might be if he frequented the public library. He feels no solemn duty toward the pocketbook and he does not feel that his intelligence is at fault if it bores him, since it has not been presented as a monument of human culture which confers superiority upon the reader.'

The pocketbook takes the hex off culture. In our particular milieu, it is a new *form* of communication. Earlier Mr. Schwartz had pointed to the fact that at college people read books because such a habit promoted communication. Later they gave up books because it interfered with normal social life. But the pocketbook permits one to return to solitary vice without interfering with one's social acceptability.

Some years back the *Partisan Review* did a study of its readers and found that they were mostly in the 18-25 group. The success of the pocketbook suggests that a saddle-shoe format for the little mag might corral a much larger group of readers.

From a somewhat different angle, it has been suggested that the current large audience for L. P. polyphony offerings is due to the technical interest in music developed by jive and bebop groups a few years back. A technical analysis and history of music in terms of written and, later, of printed scores is needed to clarify some of the relations between sight and sound. Presumably printed scores had something to do with divorcing words and music after the 16th century. But printed scores would seem to have made possible the maximal freedom of expression of 'pure music'. The visual, printed form permitted the release of the formal aspects of sound from the oral and verbal ground of music. In the same way *vers libre* was an effort to get away from the domination of printed poetry over the free oral patterns of verbal music. *Vers libristes* consciously cut back to Gregorian chant, to communal litanies and popular speech rhythms as structural base.

The habitual contemplation of the media of communication as

art forms necessarily invokes the principle that the instruments of research are also art forms, magically distorting and controlling the objects of investigation. Critical awareness of this fact has saved the modern scientist from many blunders, but such awareness has arrived tardily in the popular sphere. Naturally the great communication and entertainment trusts of North America are not eager to promote such critical awareness. The existing cultural paralysis engendered by orthodox élite-theories of culture are greatly to their advantage. But we might consider how far we have evaded the direct political control of the media by the expedient of indifference to the impact of the media so long as they can be exploited for public fun and private profit. This may prove to have been a piece of unconscious political wisdom. But so far it has been based on the dubious assumption that 'control the message and you control all'. The actual history of any of the media suggests the reverse. What is at stake is whether the new magical forms of communication are to be kept for laughs and the old forms of communication reserved for politics. Roosevelt's radio talks would have been less effective if the newspaper and editorial world had been on his side. By pretending that the new magic can he contained in the entertainment sphere we assume the old form-content split which is based on the doctrine that the form of communication is neutral. Even Hitler and Goebbels, fortunately, shared this illusion with the Western world. At present we appear to be living by an illusion but *with* magical media. Of course this may prove to be an enduring formula.

Notes on the Media as Art Forms
Marshall McLuhan - Unbound (15)

ISBN: 1-58423-051-7
Library of Congress Control Number 2005927213

Marshall McLuhan Unbound Project Editors
Eric McLuhan, W. Terrence Gordon

Published in United States in October 2005 by
Gingko Press, Inc.
5768 Paradise Drive, Suite J • Corte Madera, CA 94925
(415) 924-9615 • Fax (415) 924-9608
email: books@gingkopress.com
http://www.gingkopress.com

Design, packaging and production: Die Gestalten Verlag, Berlin
Layout and Typography: onlab, Berlin
Fonts: *Dolly* by Underware, *Bullet* by House Industries
Production: Martin Bretschneider, Vinzenz Geppert
Art direction: Robert Klanten

Made in Germany